Grief in Its Journey

KIMRA SUTTON

Foreword by Pastor Marvin Hintz
Editorial Assistance Provided by Dori Phillips

ISBN 979-8-89130-775-9 (paperback)
ISBN 979-8-89130-776-6 (digital)

Copyright © 2024 by Kimra Sutton

All rights reserved. No part of this publication may be reproduced, distributed, or transmitted in any form or by any means, including photocopying, recording, or other electronic or mechanical methods without the prior written permission of the publisher. For permission requests, solicit the publisher via the address below.

Christian Faith Publishing
832 Park Avenue
Meadville, PA 16335
www.christianfaithpublishing.com

Unless otherwise indicated, all scripture quotations are from the ESV ® Bible (The Holy Bible English Standard Version ®), copyright © 2001 by Crossway, a publishing ministry of Good News Publishers. Used by permission. All rights reserved.

Printed in the United States of America

When peace like a river attendeth my way,
When sorrows, like sea billows roll,
Whatever my lot, Thou hast taught me to say,
It is well, it is well with my soul.

For my Lord and Savior, Jesus Christ
For our children
For my late husband, Dwight; may your
kindness always live on in others.

Contents

Foreword vii
Acknowledgements xi
Introduction xiii
Chapter 1: The Shock, April 15, 2021 1
Chapter 2: God Is with Me 8
Chapter 3: Viewing Day 13
Chapter 4: Memorial Service 15
Chapter 5: Loneliness 21
Chapter 6: So Many Struggles 23
Chapter 7: Grief 27
Chapter 8: Precious Verses 34
Chapter 9: Songs 37
Chapter 10: Comfort 48
Chapter 11: Encouraging One Another 50
Chapter 12: Prayer 53
Chapter 13: Conclusion 55
Glossary of Terms 57
Take Another Step 65

Foreword

August 2006—it seemed like any other Sunday evening, but as is often the case, God was opening the book on a new, exciting, and beneficial relationship with two people who, on that evening, wandered into Delaware Bible Church.

God had brought Dwight and Kimra into my sphere of acquaintances, and what transpired in the sixteen years that followed was, without a doubt, a friendship that is filled with repeated evidences of the Lord's grace and goodness.

Until my retirement in 2013, I had the privilege of being Dwight and Kimra's pastor. It was within that context that I witnessed God at work in their lives. The external evidences included the time of their dating, premarital counseling, and officiating at their wedding. It also included watching them gain greater financial freedom that enabled them to first rent and then purchase their first home. In both the rental and the purchased home, I was invited to gather with them and other family and friends to pray a prayer of dedication over the home that God had provided for them.

The internal evidences included a growing commitment to the Lord as seen in their character, their service, and their devotion for one another and family members. Though external, Dwight's growing faith and commitment were apparent at his baptism, which I was honored to perform.

On April 15, 2021, God chose to call Dwight home to heaven! Kimra has chosen to record the path that Dwight's passing has brought. In it one finds reality rather than pious platitudes. But in addition to reality, one finds evidence of our God, who is faithful at all times and whose faithfulness is most evident during the deepest valleys of life. This truth itself has the potential of being yet another pious platitude. What the reader finds in Kimra's account is one who chooses to lean into the truth of God found in his Word and, in so doing, experiences the comfort, faithfulness, and love of God.

What follows is an extremely practical, honest, and scriptural record of Kimra's journey through grief. It is a gripping testimony of a loving Abba (Father) who is true to his promise to never leave or forsake and who is more than sufficient to be a comforter to all who will come to him.

Pastor Marvin Hintz
Galatians 6:14

It is my hope and prayer that every person who reads this book will experience the love and comfort I have experienced from my Heavenly Father.

Acknowledgements

I would like to take this opportunity to thank so many who have walked with me during my grief journey and the writing of this book.

First and foremost, I thank my Heavenly Father, my Abba, for being the one constant in my life. He used so many to love, comfort, and encourage me during this journey.

For my loving husband, Dwight, who gave me sixteen years of love, joy, laughter, and support and whose passing is the reason I wrote this book.

For my six children and their better halves, thank you for being with me every step of the way and for my sixteen grandbabies who bring me laughter and love.

For my siblings who have been there for me in the highs and lows.

For my sweet Aunt Nancy who has been a dedicated prayer warrior for me as I have walked this journey and wrote this book.

For my dear girlfriends, Janet and LouAnn, for your shoulders to cry on and for the laughter, prayers, and friendship.

For my sweet sisterhood, for our walks, talks, times of prayer and meals together, and your friendship.

For my dear friend, Lori, for your counsel, love, support, friendship, and prayers.

For my Delaware Bible Church family—I love you all and couldn't have done this without you! And for Pastors Marv, Scott, Brad, and Aaron, for your leadership, care, and prayers.

For my Mountainside Bible Chapel family in Schroon Lake, for your encouragement, support, love, and prayers. So grateful for you all.

For my daughter, Lauren, and my friend, Beth, who helped proofread this document, and for my friend, Dori, who did the editing. I couldn't have finished this book without all of you!

For my parents, Paul and Sally Lang, who raised me to know Jesus. Can't wait to celebrate Jesus with you one day.

For my "adopted" mom, Janice Davis, for loving me, "talking God" with me, and for all your prayers.

Last but not least, for my cousin Jane Seiling, for pushing me to write this book. Thank you for all your support and step-by-step help. And for her husband, Bill, for cheering me on.

I would like to give a huge thank-you to Milt for his support and encouragement. If it wasn't for you, this book would not have happened. I love you!

Introduction

May 26, 2007, is the day Dwight and I were joined in marriage, creating a home for our five teenagers and for our oldest to visit. Dwight was the kind of husband I had always wanted, the father for our kids that I will be forever grateful for. He was funny, joyful, a keeper of odd knowledge, loving, and firm. He loved Jesus, his family, his friends, and me. He was the love of my life.

We loved being together: doing yard work, renovating our home, working on projects, etc. We loved to travel and watch *The History Underground* and *Murdoch Mysteries* together. My favorite thing was to sit next to him in our pickup truck. I loved snuggling up beside him, talking, and just being with him. He said, "We will do this until we don't have a truck anymore." I sat next to him for thirteen years.

My pet names for him were "my love" and "honey." His pet names for me were "babe" and "honey." The love we shared was demonstrated by our actions and words. We were always supportive of each other. We chose to love each other every day, in the good times and the rough times. We were able to do this with God's help; he was our first love. That is why we worked so well together. God was first, then each other, and then ourselves.

As our children got married and more grandkids started coming, the joy in his step was sweet to see. We had three older adult grandchildren whom we saw occasionally. Two of them started families, so we had three great-granddaughters as well. We video chatted with the grandbabies who lived out of state. I loved to watch Papa interact with the grands. He would teach the younger ones how to play a game or put together a puzzle. But on the top of his list was planting flowers. To this day, our granddaughter, Dixie, still talks about planting flowers with her Papa.

Dwight Leroy Sutton was everything, and more, I could have asked for in a husband and father. He loved me and our children unconditionally, just like Jesus. What more could I want?

The Shock, April 15, 2021

> For God alone my soul waits in silence; from him comes my salvation. He alone is my rock and my salvation, my fortress; I shall not be greatly shaken. (Psalm 62:1–2)

When I woke up at 4:50 a.m. for my morning bathroom run, my husband Dwight was already up. I looked out into the living room; it was so dark and uninviting. Assuming my industrious husband was outside watering the flowers and having a smoke, I settled back into bed and fell fast asleep. Little did I know it would be the last good night's sleep I would have for a very long time.

At 6:55 a.m., I woke up. "Good morning, Heavenly Father!" I said aloud. After reciting Psalm 118:24, "This is the day that the Lord has made; let us rejoice and be glad in it," I sat up. I put my feet on the floor and unplugged my phone and lamp cord. As I headed toward the bedroom door, I was so excited. Dwight and I had plans to take our grown daughters, Lindsey and Lauren, and our three grandbabies to the zoo!

When I opened the bedroom door, I noticed Dwight was lying in the recliner with his eyes closed. I tilted my head from left to right, then stopped in wonder. True, his eyes were closed, but his mouth was open. And although his left arm was lying across his chest, his right arm was dangling off the right side of the recliner. "Father, I think you have Dwight with you," I said out loud. But then I thought, *No, he could just be asleep.* As I headed to the bathroom, I decided not to flush the toilet so I wouldn't wake him. When I exited the bathroom, I looked at Dwight again. He was still in the same position. I continued to walk into the living room and noticed the TV was on. I turned it off and stood close to Dwight. It was then that I realized that he was dead; his soul was with our Lord and Savior. Tears started streaming down my face, and I talked with my Heavenly Father: "Thank you for bringing Dwight and I together and giving us the best sixteen years of friendship and fourteen years of marriage. Thank you for the confirmation of Dwight's salvation just one month ago! Oh, how that brings me comfort!" As I stood there, God's peace washed over me.

Then I turned my conversation to Dwight: "Thank you for choosing me! Thank you for all the love and laughter these past sixteen years. I will miss you so much!" The tears turned into a torrent as I continued: "Thank you for being a wonderful dad to all six of our children and a doting grandpa to our seven grandchildren and one great-granddaughter! Thank you for sharing your love with them, no matter what was going on in their lives. They will miss you!"

Then it hit me; I had things to do. Focusing back on my Heavenly Father, I said, "Father, I have to wake my girls and call our other four kids. I need to call 911 and my church. I can't do this without you. Please give me the strength!" As I looked at my pajamas, I thought to myself, *I don't want anyone to see me like this!* So I got dressed and washed my face. While I was looking in the mirror to put my hair up, it dawned on me that I should check Dwight for a pulse, just in case. "Oh, Father, help me!" I pleaded. "I have never touched a dead body before!" Having worked in Early Childhood over the past twenty-five years, I had taken many CPR and first-aid classes, so I knew what to do. As I touched Dwight's inner wrist, I was alarmed by how cold and stiff he was. The placement of the remote caught my eye; it was perfectly positioned on the right arm of the chair. I put my finger under his nose: no air. I looked at his chest; it was not rising. The tears came like a flood and trickled down my face again. I rubbed his head like I always did while we were lying in bed. "I love you, Dwight!" I declared confidently. Then turned my conversation to God. "Father, I need you! I want to heal well and heal well for you!" I wasn't sure what that looked like, just that I wanted it. Proverbs 3:5–6 popped into my head, and I said it out loud as I continued to sob: "Trust in the Lord with all your heart, and do not lean on your own understanding. In all your ways acknowledge him, and he will make straight your path." I wiped my face with the back of my hand and said, "Father, let's do this!"

As I walked up the stairs, I debated who to wake first: Lindsey or Lauren. I decided to wake Lauren first, since she didn't have children sleeping in the room with her. When I entered the room, she was still sleeping. I asked the Father to give me the words to make my delivery clear. "Lauren, can you wake up?" I gently implored. She opened her eyes and looked at me. "You need to sit up. I have something to tell you."

"What's wrong?" she asked through sleepy eyes. Trying not to lose control, these words came out: "Dwight went to be with Jesus. He is downstairs and lying peacefully in his recliner." She responded with alarm, "What?" I repeated my delivery and told her to sit up and take a few minutes to let the reality sink in. She sat up and the tears started flowing down her face. Then she asked, "What do you need me to do?" I asked her to get Lindsey and meet me by the stairs.

Lindsey came rushing toward me. "What's wrong?" she asked. I held her hands and repeated the words I had shared with Lauren: "Dwight went to be with Jesus. He is downstairs and lying peacefully in his recliner." She cried along with Lauren. "I need to call 911," I told them.

"Can I see him?" Lindsey asked. "No," I said firmly. "Just know that he looks peaceful. I want you to remember him the way he was yesterday." She nodded, as I continued, "I am going to call 911, and then I will come back up."

I headed outside to the front yard. "Okay, Father. Help me to speak clearly so the dispatcher can understand me." I entered 911 on my cell phone, and a young man answered the line: "911, this is so-and-so. What is your emergency?"

I took a deep breath and replied, "Hi, my name is Kimra Sutton. I woke up around 7:00 a.m. and found my husband, Dwight Sutton, dead in his recliner." He asked where I lived, if there were any other people in the house, and if I was okay. "I live at 26 Pleasant Court.

Yes, my two daughters and three grandkids are here. Can you please ask the EMS to turn off their sirens before they get here? I don't want to wake the grandchildren just yet. And yes, I am okay. I cried before I called you because I wanted to be able to speak clearly when I called."

As I was walking up and down the sidewalk, my neighbor Chantel came out of her house and headed for her car. I walked over to let her know about Dwight. She was shocked but said she and her boys would be over to help out in any way they could.

After getting off the phone, I headed back inside. I told the girls that the EMS would be arriving soon. Lauren asked if she could call my son-in-law Caleb, and I gave her the go-ahead.

The EMS arrived and I went outside to meet the two men. I introduced myself and brought them downstairs. They saw Dwight lying in his recliner. I walked over to him and rubbed his head while I shared the events of the last few hours. I heard a knock at the door; it was two police officers. I brought them down, and the two EMS workers left. I shared, once again, the order of events. By now it was about 7:50 a.m. "Would it be okay if I went upstairs to be with my girls?" I inquired. "We need to call the other kids." The police officer replied, "Yes, go ahead. We need to check things out down here."

As I started up the stairs, I felt like I might collapse. I wanted to cry. I wished it was all a dream! But I had to stay strong. I was in shock, but I was functioning. As I climbed the stairs, I knew this was real. When I got to the top of the stairs, I called my friend, Monnette to come help with the grandbabies so Lindsey and Lauren could get a little time to grieve.

Next, I called my son, Corey. Oh, the shock that hit him when I told him that Dwight was gone! He started to throw things and cried, "It just can't be true!" Once he calmed down, he, his girlfriend, and my granddaughter came over. Then I called my son-in-law Seth. He responded in shock and disbelief but said he would notify my daughter, Laura.

About this time, the coroner showed up. I went out front to meet him. He was a caring man and asked me if I was okay. "To the best of my ability," I replied. He asked if I wanted to talk to my doctor and the head coroner. I agreed. He called the doctor and handed the phone to me. I shared with him what had happened. The doctor reminded me that Dwight had cholesterol issues. He presumed that Dwight had died from a massive heart attack. He ended the conversation with, "If you need anything, call me." I thanked him, said goodbye, and handed the phone back to the coroner.

Just then, my phone rang. It was our daughter, Tori. Her husband, Caleb, had told her about Dwight's passing. She was crying so hard! "What happened?" she asked. I told her how I had found her dad resting peacefully in the recliner. I shared that the doctor thought he had probably died from a heart attack and told her that the police and coroner were here. She assured me that they were on their way. "I love you! See you soon," I replied.

Around 9:00 a.m., the investigator coroner showed up. We talked out front, and once again, I shared the events of the morning. Then I showed him inside.

Shortly afterward, Laura arrived. She was standing in the entryway, and she was very upset. I went to her and wrapped my arms around her. Then it dawned on me. "Laura, what door did you come through?" She responded, "The back way—through your room. Mom, I saw him! No one told me not to come in that way!" She sobbed. "Oh, Laura, I am so sorry!" I replied as I squeezed her tightly. We walked upstairs. By this time, five of the kids and one son-in-love had gathered together at the house: Lindsey, Corey, Lauren, Laura, Tori, and Caleb. Tori asked if she could call the last sibling, Angie, and I agreed.

I went downstairs to get a sweatshirt and noticed that the coroner was gone; however, there was still one police officer and the investigator present. The police officer informed me that they were just waiting on the transporter to arrive. Dwight would be taken to Dayton for an autopsy.

I headed back upstairs to make another phone call. This one was going to be the hardest. I had to call Dwight's only sibling, his sister, Marilyn. My throat was dry as her phone rang. When she picked up, tears flooded my eyes. As I shared how I had found Dwight dead in his recliner, my heart broke for her. As she cried, I shared with her what the doctor had said. We agreed that she would contact the cousins.

My next call was to my church. The church secretary, Jessica, answered—she was amazing! She was so helpful. She offered to post our family's loss on the church prayer page and start a meal train. I thanked her and asked her to please tell our pastors. Within fifteen to twenty minutes after we hung up, Pastor Scott was at my door.

After calling the church, I called my siblings. I got ahold of Ronda, and she called Marla and David. Sharla called me, so I repeated the sequence of events to her.

By 10:00 a.m., our church family started arriving. Many people brought fruit baskets or food throughout the day and into the evening. As I shared the same information over and over, I started to feel like I was living in space. I felt like I was floating, and it was all just a bad dream.

Around 10:30 a.m., the transporter arrived. A couple of minutes later, the police officer said they would be bringing Dwight upstairs. Tori asked if she could see him as they took him outside. I looked at her, held her hands, and said, "Trust me, you don't want that to be your last memory of him. Remember him alive and laughing. You can see him at the viewing." I told the police officer to tell the transporter that he could go. I hugged Tori, and we cried together.

I met the police officer out front. Shaking his hand, I thanked him for taking care of Dwight and us. "It was my privilege to be here and serve you," he replied. "I could tell you were Christians by the way you talked and how close you were as a family." Now, that is what I always want people to see: Jesus!

After he left, I went back inside the apartment—our apartment. Dwight's chair was there; his belongings were there, but he was not. I asked Pastor Scott to come downstairs and take Dwight's chair away. I cried, but there was no way I could keep it. The apartment felt so empty! I felt so empty. I took a deep breath. Life would never be the same.

As people came and went, I felt so blessed to have them with me. The love of Christ was shown to me in so many wonderful ways.

However, at times, I would stare off into space, and then come back to the present, not really thinking. I just felt so numb.

My sweet five-year-old granddaughter came over to me and said, "I know why you are so sad, Grandma Kimmi. Because Papa died and is with Jesus." I gave her a hug and replied, "Yes, I am sad. I will miss Papa a lot. But he is with Jesus and that is a great place for him to be." She hugged me back and then left to go play. I look back on this interaction with her fondly. She knew where Papa was and that we would see him again! A year later she accepted Jesus into her heart and was baptized. Her Papa would have been so tickled with her decision.

My close friends gathered downstairs with me from around 7:00 to 11:00 p.m. We shared memories, laughed, and cried together. My friend, Steve, made arrangements to have bagpipers play "Amazing Grace" at the end of the military services. The overwhelming care and love shown to me by our friends left me awestruck.

After everyone left, I thought, *Now what?* I hesitantly went back downstairs into our bedroom and looked around. The tears started falling again. I put on my pj's, grabbed one of Dwight's T-shirts, crawled into bed, and bawled. I called out to my Father, "Please, God, comfort me! I can't do this without you. You are my rock and my salvation. You said in your Word that you won't leave me or forsake me. My heart hurts. It feels like it is going to break! Oh, Father, wrap me in your loving arms!" As I was praying, my body felt warm, and I knew God was with me. For the next hour and a half, I read and answered about ten to fifteen messages. Around 1:30 a.m., I decided to close my eyes and asked God to help me sleep.

God Is with Me

> Even though I walk through the valley of the shadow of death, I will fear no evil, for you are with me; your rod and your staff, they comfort me. (Psalm 23:4)

The next seven days were so hard! I was foggy. I was numb. I was dazed by grief. And yet we were so blessed as people continued to provide meals and stopped by to check on us. Lindsey and Lauren took care of the kids, and even I jumped in from time to time to distract me from the reality of Dwight's passing.

I remember waking up on Friday and going through my normal morning routine—reciting Psalm 118:24, unplugging my phone and lamp cords, making the bed, and getting dressed. I felt like a robot. When it came time to go upstairs, I looked at the bedroom door that led to the living room, but also to the door that led outside. I was so torn. I really didn't want to open the door that led to the living room, because it felt like I would find Dwight in his recliner all over again. My stomach was in knots! I knew I wouldn't be able to avoid opening the bedroom door forever, so I prayed: "Father, I know you have me. We can do this!" I opened the door and walked forward—we made it!

Around lunchtime, my sweet friend and sister in Christ, Lori, came bearing gifts of paper plates and plastic utensils to limit the need to wash dishes—such practical help! We went down into my apartment to visit. She immediately noticed Dwight's chair was gone. I told her that it would have been too hard to keep it. I also shared with her my dilemma regarding which door to use. She was happy to hear that I had leaned on God and was able to walk through the doorway into the living room. I asked her what she thought about me getting biblical counseling, and she agreed that it was a good idea. "Great!" I responded. "I have the book all picked out. When should we start?" She laughed and said, "You would be the one to pick out your own book." We set a date to meet after I returned from the wedding of Dwight's second cousin in Georgia. Honestly, I think those were the best two decisions I made: going to the wedding and getting counseling.

Nighttime came. I read my Bible, listened to music, and answered messages. Then I crawled into bed and cried as I cradled Dwight's T-shirt, breathing in the scent of his body. I finally fell asleep around 1:00 a.m.

Saturday morning came all too early. I awoke and executed my morning routine. When I grabbed the bedroom door handle, I whispered, "Father, here we go again." I opened the door and took a step forward. "We made it, Father! Thank you!" I exclaimed.

Later that morning, Angie, Tori, Corey and Laura came over. It was so wonderful to have them there, along with Lindsey and Lauren. We shared memories, laughed and cried together. As I listened to their stories, I thought how awed Dwight would have been to hear how he had touched each of their lives. They worked together to finish the obituary and collect pictures for a posterboard display. To this day, I am honored to have these six in my life.

I left a little before noon and went to the funeral home to meet Mike, the funeral director, and Pastor Hintz. We talked about Dwight's body being back from the autopsy. I picked out a book and thank-you notes, and we talked in general. Mike made me feel so comfortable and Pastor Hintz was a welcomed "familiar face." As I walked out, my mind was so foggy. I couldn't believe I was doing this: making funeral arrangements for the love of my life.

When I returned, the kids picked out some pictures and sent in the obituary. After those details were completed, we were able to just enjoy being together. The laughter filled my heart.

That night, after I put on my pj's, I read God's Word, prayed, and listened to music. I held Dwight's T-shirt tightly as I cried. Around 1:00 a.m., sleep finally came.

The next morning, I got up to go to church and Sunday School. It would feel good to be in God's house with my friends, I reasoned. However, when I arrived, the thought of walking through the doors of the church—knowing that Dwight would never walk through those doors again—crushed me. My steps were heavy, and I felt nauseated, the closer I got to the door. I wasn't sure if I was going to make it. In God's strength, I was able to walk through the doors. My friends greeted me with much love, hugs, and smiles. They asked what they could do for me and shared their memories of Dwight. It was a little overwhelming but just what I needed. It did feel good to be in God's house with my friends, but it just wasn't the same without Dwight with me. I missed him so much!

I sat with my friend, Rachel, in the back. As we sang, I cried and swayed back and forth. I continued to cry outwardly, but in my heart, I praised the Lord. Rachel comforted me by putting her arm around me. It was such a blessing to have her by my side.

I stayed focused for about twenty minutes while I took notes. As my mind drifted back to Dwight, I reminisced about the first time we attended Delaware Bible Church; saying "I do" on the same platform Pastor Scott was preaching from; and singing up front with a group of friends at Christmastime. Next, I remembered the church honoring our veterans by having them come up front. In my mind's eye, I could see Dwight getting up from his seat and heading up front when they played the army theme song. I finally came back to the present to hear Pastor Scott coming to the conclusion of his sermon. Then my thoughts wandered to the upcoming viewing, as well as the memorial and military services. Tears fell like giant raindrops onto my notebook. The reality that Dwight's last time in our church would be for his funeral, was gut-wrenching. We had created so many friendships and memories over our fifteen years there!

As I drove home, I thought, *Thank you, God, for the strength and the love you showed me through the body of Christ.* It was hard not *having Dwight with me, but I know he is with you. I am okay because I know where he is, and I know you are with me.*

That night I noticed my heart was hurting to the point that I thought I might be having a heart attack. I took a couple of deep breaths and realized my heart hurt because I was missing the love of my life. My heart felt like it was breaking because I missed his voice, his touch. I missed hearing him say that he loved me. I missed his laughter and kisses. I missed packing his lunch and preparing his coffee for the morning. That pain in my heart truly represented the love that we shared being ripped away.

Monday, the girls, grandkids, and I went downtown to the library. We walked around town and stopped to get something to drink. It was a lowkey kind of day. Later that afternoon, Laura came over and hung out. That evening, Tori, Caleb, and friends came over to hang out with Lindsey and Lauren.

That night, I read my Bible and prayed. I listened to music. I cried as I clung to Dwight's T-shirt. Sleep came around 12:30 a.m.

I woke up excited that my friends Rob, Becky, and their daughter were coming to visit. As I got up and got dressed, I thanked the Lord for the day ahead. Then I headed upstairs to eat breakfast with the girls and grandkids.

Rob, Becky, and "E" arrived with lunch around 12:30 p.m. We had the best time. The kids played together while we adults chatted. My dear friend Janet popped over for a little bit too. Everyone headed home around 5:00 p.m. My heart was so full of love and comfort.

That night I started reading Psalm 23. I listened to music and answered text messages. I held onto Dwight's T-shirt and prayed as the tears fell. The last thing I remember seeing on my phone was that it was midnight.

Wednesday morning, I recited Psalm 118:24 and unplugged my phone and lamp as usual. However, as I was getting dressed, I noticed the pitter-patter of little feet running around upstairs. I quickly finished dressing and went upstairs to find out what was going on. The grandkids were all excited because their dads were going to be arriving soon! We had some breakfast, the kids played, and we cleaned up the kitchen. Before we knew it, Joe and Derek had arrived. We were so glad they were with us. The rest of the day was spent just hanging out together.

That evening, I worked on putting pictures on posterboard and collecting items to take to the church for Dwight's memorial service. As I finished, I was so exhausted! My thoughts turned to what was coming over the next few days. Then I crawled into bed, listened to music, read Psalm 23, and prayed. Clutching Dwight's T-shirt, I fell asleep around 11:30 p.m.

Thursday morning, I woke up feeling a little more rested. I recited Psalm 118:24, unplugged everything, got dressed, and asked God to hold me up. All of a sudden, I felt very off! After talking to the kids about it, Joe suggested that I might be dehydrated. He encouraged me to keep drinking water throughout the morning. By late afternoon, I had downed four bottles of water and was feeling much better.

Around 5:30 p.m., all the kids and grandkids arrived. I took pictures all evening. Everyone was eating, playing corn hole, and laughing together. Later, we enjoyed a bonfire and s'mores at the firepit which Dwight had finished building just five days before he died. It was truly a treasure to have the family gathered around it!

My sisters Marla and Sharla, brother-in-love, Jeff, and nephew Logan arrived a few hours later. I went over to greet them with a hug, but no words came, only tears. It was so good to hold them close.

By the time the evening came to an end, I was so mentally and physically tired. I snuggled under my sheet and blanket that night; my brain felt like mush. The sorrow was so heavy, and my heart still hurt. I sent a verbal letter heavenward: "Oh, Father, I am lying here, struggling! I need you! Please be with me. I need to be able to function—no, I want more than that! I want to show your love tomorrow. Please, give me what I need! Love, your daughter." As I was holding Dwight's T-shirt, I drifted off to sleep. The time was 12:30 p.m.

Viewing Day

> This is the day that the Lord has made; let
> us rejoice and be glad in it. (Psalm 118:24)

I woke up quoting Psalm 118:24, "This is the day that the Lord has made; let us rejoice and be glad in it." I continued, conversing with my Heavenly Father: "Abba, I need your strength, Your comfort...your grace. Give me the stamina I need to greet people. May my words glorify you. I love you."

I started the day by going out to Fresh Start with my sisters. It's honestly a blur, but I do know I am grateful we were together. Around 11:00 a.m., Derek, Joe, and I collected the items for display: the pictures, the coffee table and key holder that Dwight had made, his baby shoes, his lunch box and safety vest, his coffee cup, the books he liked, the Browns and Indians sweatshirt and coat, his ball caps, etc. There were about seven areas set up to display these remembrances. I wanted to make sure I represented well who he was.

My emotions were all over the place as I was getting ready. I already had picked out my dress; it was orange and white checkered. (Dwight used to call it my tablecloth dress!) As I finished getting ready, I begged God to go before me. "Please help me not to lose it when I see Dwight lying in the casket!" I pleaded.

We all headed to the church. As I drove, my body felt heavy, my brain was racing, and my heart continued to hurt. I wanted to turn around and go back home! After pulling into the parking lot, I sat there for a few seconds and took several deep breaths.

I walked into the church with my family and was greeted by the funeral home workers and my pastors. I thanked them all for being there for us. I waited for all my kids to arrive before I went in to see Dwight. We entered the sanctuary together and gathered around the casket. I remember saying to Dwight, "I love you and miss you so much! I am grateful for you. Enjoy being with Jesus." Tears fell as I laid my hand on his arm. I took a step back so the kids could take their turn being at the casket. There were lots of hugs and tears.

People started showing up to pay their respects from 3:00 to 5:00 p.m. At 5:00 p.m., we took a dinner break. The family of Gary Fickle, a friend of Dwight, was kind enough to provide a meal for us. They wanted to support us in the same way that we had supported them when Gary went home to be with the Lord seven months prior. I was so blessed by their help. I was also glad to have the opportunity to reminisce with Dwight's cousins, Charles, and his daughter, Chandra, from Rochester, New York. After an hour, it was time for "round two" of visitation. People were waiting to see us in the lobby. The doors opened, and I shot up a prayer, "Okay, Father, you've got me!" As each one approached me, memories would overwhelm me. Our conversations were warm, caring, and loving. Without realizing it, I found myself reaching into the casket to rub Dwight's shirt. I guess it gave me comfort while I talked with people. It was all very draining emotionally and physically.

After everyone had left, I asked the family to join me in prayer. We gathered in a circle and held hands. As we bowed our heads, I thanked the Lord for Dwight's life and his love for each of us. I also thanked the Lord for his love that he demonstrated by dying on the cross to take away our sins. In closing, I added, "Please give us all a good night's sleep! Amen." We hugged some more. Everyone was heading out, but I decided to stop at the casket one more time. I put my hand on Dwight's arm and just stood there, tears falling. I felt so sad! I missed him so much!

Once we got home, Lindsey, Derek, Lauren, and Joe put their children to bed. We chatted briefly before heading to our rooms, exhausted. I lay in bed crying and holding Dwight's T-shirt close to my body, smelling it. I asked God to wrap his arms of love around me. I cried and cried, until I fell asleep.

Memorial Service

> For God so loved the world, that he gave his
> only Son, that whoever believes in him should
> not perish but have eternal life. (John 3:16)

I woke up Saturday, April 24, 2021, went through my normal routine, and talked to my Heavenly Father. I felt so heavy and drained. I forced myself to open the bedroom door, pushing the memory of Dwight in his recliner out of my mind. I had to "stuff" that memory in order to keep living in the house.

I went through the motions of showering, fixing my hair, and dressing. I felt like a robot, functioning without thought. Upstairs, the house was buzzing with activity. I could hear the little feet of my grandbabies on the floor above me. The thought of them brought a smile to my face. But then a shadow of sadness washed over me when I thought of those beautiful children without their Papa or Grandpa here anymore.

I arrived at the church around 9:30 a.m. They had moved Dwight, the pictures, and other memorabilia into the commons. I went over to him, rubbed his shirt, and told him I loved him.

People started arriving around 10:00 a.m. to pay their respects. Again, kindness, love, and hugs were bestowed on our family. I walked around greeting people and keeping busy.

At one point, Katie from the funeral home asked me if I had pallbearers. When I asked her how many I could have, she replied, "Six would be good."

"How about nine?" I countered, and she agreed. I gathered my son, Corey, five sons-in-love—Derek, Joe, Ken, Caleb, and Seth—as well as my three nephews, Logan, Paul, and Cody. "Thank you for doing this," I told them. "He loved each and every one of you." Katie then proceeded to give them instructions.

I found the gentleman in charge of the military services and thanked him. I shared with him how much Dwight loved his country. He handed me a coin that represented Dwight's being a veteran, and me, his widow.

Before going in for the service, Katie gathered our family together beside the casket so everyone could say their last goodbyes. There was a lot of crying and hugging. As I approached the casket to share my final words with the love of my life, so many memories came to mind! One fond memory was how Dwight used to tell me that he loved me "BLYs," which stood for Buzz Lightyear, meaning to infinity and beyond! Yes, that would be my fond farewell to him. "I love you BLYs! I miss you so much, but I will be okay because I have God. Enjoy being with Jesus, Dwight. I will see you again in heaven," I whispered, choking back the tears.

Katie invited us to tuck him in. She closed the lid of the casket, and we spread the flag across the top. Tears fell from all our faces. My sons-in-love wrapped their arms around their wives, our daughters, and my son held onto his daughter, Dixie. Katie and an assistant pushed the casket up the aisle into the sanctuary. Pastor Scott and I followed behind and my children and grandchildren followed us. Once we were all seated, the service began.

It was so amazing to see the army veterans and active-duty servicemen pass by me, stop at the casket, salute, and walk out of the sanctuary. I had no idea that they were going to honor Dwight in this way. I was in awe and so thankful that Dwight had faithfully served his country which he loved.

Pastor Scott greeted everyone on behalf of our family and thanked them for being with us. Dwight had highlighted Psalm 27:1 in his Apologetics Study Bible: "The Lord is my light and my salvation; whom shall I fear? The Lord is the stronghold of my life; of whom shall I be afraid?" I had been memorizing this verse for two months, not realizing that Dwight had highlighted it in his Bible. I sent up a little "God wink" at the thought. Pastor Scott went on to explain that Delaware Bible Church had two goals at this memorial service: (1) to honor Dwight's memory, and (2) to honor God for what he had done in and through his life.

We stood and sang "He Leadeth Me." I picked this song because Dwight was such a faithful follower of God who led him. The chorus goes like this: "He leadeth me, he leadeth me, by his own hand he leadeth me; his faithful follower I would be, for by his hand he leadeth me."

Everyone sat down and Allen Mecklenberg sang "Broken Road." Allen and Dwight had become good friends over the fifteen years we attended Delaware Bible Church. The first time we saw him sing, we called him "the opera man." I was so grateful that Alan agreed to sing at Dwight's memorial service.

Family and friends stood up to share memories. So many sweet things were said about Dwight. Our daughter, Lindsey, commented that it is never too late, referring to Dwight being fifty-two years old when we got married and willingly taking on four more kids. He was so brave, and he saw the value in things. It's never too late, and relationships are worth taking the time. Dwight did that.

Pastor Hintz shared some thoughtful words. He talked about the phrase "In the beginning, God..." He said that's how he thought of my relationship with Dwight. From the beginning, our relationship was centered on God. He then referenced the book of Ruth and the phrase "It just happened that Ruth came to the fields of Boaz." It just happened because of God! In our case, I was living at Silver Maple Apartments and Dwight was the maintenance man. Pastor mentioned how we would take walks in the neighborhood, and we "just happened" to walk by Delaware Bible Church. We started attending DBC in August 2006, and he officiated our wedding standing on that very same platform on May 26, 2007. On a lighter note, he shared about the Cubs tie Dwight had given him to wear at the wedding, while Dwight wore his Cleveland Indians tie. Pastor was wearing his Cubs tie at the memorial service to honor not just a wonderful man, but an amazing Christian brother.

As I listened to these words and so many more, I laughed, tears fell, and my soul was full of love. I felt the sweet presence of our loving God. Pastor continued to share about Dwight's testimony and his baptism. He had become a role model and his sacrifice of hard work provided for our family. Dwight loved by his actions. He loved all his children and family this way. In closing, Pastor referred back to the phrase, "In the beginning, God…"

"What God begins, he also finishes. He is the Alpha, the beginning, and the Omega, the end. Dwight's passing didn't take God by surprise. God, in his goodness, prepares us. We have been so blessed by Dwight. We thank him for being a provider, a husband, a father, and a friend. Dwight, your life, your example, have contributed significantly to our lives to become better people."

We stood to sing the final two songs, "In the Garden" and "It Is Well with My Soul," which were led by our sweet friends, Jason and Chelsea Jones. Oh, how the tears fell as I swayed back and forth! I praised the Lord through song, even though my heart ached, and my body was numb.

Pastor Scott closed the service honoring the Lord. He shared about the Garden of Eden in Genesis 2 where God walked with man. Then in chapter 3, sin separated man from God! "God is holy and perfectly free from sin," he explained. He continued by describing who Jesus is—a shepherd who loves and guides us. Jesus was sent to earth to be born as a baby to initiate a rescue mission. Pastor then turned our attention to John 3, where Nicodemus is wondering who Jesus is. There, Jesus states, "Truly, truly, I say to you, unless one is born again he cannot see the kingdom of God." Pastor shared John 3:16, "For God so loved the world that he gave his only Son, that whoever believes in him should not perish but have eternal life." He said that God doesn't worry about your past; he is concerned about your eternal life.

(How would you answer the question "Are you spending eternity in heaven with a loving God or in hell with Satan, a deceitful liar?" The gospel is so sweet! Consider researching it for yourself and really look into who God is.)

Pastor closed with Psalm 23:6, "Surely goodness and mercy shall follow me all the days of my life, and I shall dwell in the house of the Lord forever."

After he closed in prayer, we followed Dwight's casket outside to the parking lot. It was breezy and cool. As I stood next to the casket, just staring at it, I withdrew into my own little world. I cried really hard and rocked back and forth.

A reading was done by the gentleman in charge of the military service. He gave me a copy of it later. The twenty-one-gun salute was next. I jumped each time the guns went off! As the two active-duty servicemen folded the flag, it dawned on me that they were going to present it to me. "Oh, Father, hold me tight!" I pleaded. The serviceman presented the flag to me, giving me his condolences. I bawled as I thanked him and hugged the flag close to my heart. It was so surreal—like I was in a movie—but it was very real. To close the military service, "Amazing Grace" was played on the bagpipes. The music continued as people loved on me and gave me hugs.

When the pallbearers were called to carry Dwight's casket to the hearse, the finality of it all really hit me. He was gone and would not be coming back to me! I stood there in a daze, watching until the door closed and the vehicle pulled away.

All of a sudden, I came back to the present. People were telling me that they weren't staying for lunch but that they would see me later. I announced, "I am hungry. Let's go eat!" I guess grief does weird things to you sometimes!

After the meal was over and the people were gone, I went back into the sanctuary. As I stood there, the memories of our times together in this church started flooding over me: Dwight and I attending our first service, potlucks, taking communion together, attending Sunday School, getting married, all the friendships, and how we had just celebrated his life. I was tired and sad, and I wondered, "What does God have next for me?"

I drove home by myself in a dazed fog, with a broken heart, but thanking God for being with me. Once I arrived home, I went downstairs to my apartment. Dwight's things from the service were in my living room. I looked at them. Feeling numb, I went into my bedroom and changed my clothes. I sat on the edge of my bed, feeling like I was in a twilight zone; nothing seemed real. I snapped out of it and heard the chatter coming from my family upstairs. I asked God for strength to join them.

As I took each step, my heart was buoyed by the laughter upstairs. I knew Dwight would want me to enjoy being with them. We took pictures so I would have them to look back on, which I have many times since Dwight's passing. The grandkids have grown, and we have four new ones, plus a grandson on the way. Papa Dwight would have enjoyed each and every one of them.

As everyone started leaving, my heart was sad, and my body hurt. I was so grateful that Joe, Lauren, and their daughter stayed an extra night. I knew tomorrow night I would be alone, but for tonight, I still had family close by.

I retired for the night. Holding Dwight's T-shirt, I cried so hard that my eyes hurt. I talked to God about how much I missed my love and the hurt I was feeling. I put on some music, answered some texts, and cried some more—finally falling asleep sometime after 1:00 a.m.

Sunday morning around 8:00 a.m., Joe, Lauren, and my granddaughter left to head back home. Hugs, tears, and "I love you's" exchanged, I turned and went inside. I was by myself…now what?

Loneliness

> For the Lord is good; his steadfast love endures forever, and his faithfulness to all generations. (Psalm 100:5)

Loneliness—oh, what a challenge! Loneliness can cause so many emotions, but for me, it caused depression. I found myself coming home, only to walk around the house, touching the walls and the furniture Dwight had built, then sitting on the steps to cry. I felt so alone in this world. I slept a lot.

On July 12, I was reading *A Small Book for the Hurting Heart*, written by Paul Tautges. Day 43 quoted Isaiah 43:2, "When you pass through the waters, I will be with you; and through the rivers, they shall not overwhelm you; when you walk through fire you shall not be burned, and the flame shall not consume you." Paul continued: "Comfort from God does not only come to us after our trial has come to an end, or after we have accepted that it may never end (in this life), but rather, the comfort of God's presence is with us during our times of grief and loss. The realization of God's presence is not determined by our emotions, but by embracing scriptural promises by faith, promises like the one quoted above."

Now when I am lonely, I talk to my Heavenly Father and read his Word. Don't get me wrong; after twenty-two months, I still feel lonely, but it isn't as bad because I know that my God is with me all the time.

The following is an excerpt from my grief study, Week 5:
Where is God in your loneliness? Write a letter to God telling him about your struggles with loneliness.

Abba,

You and I have had many conversations about my struggles with loneliness over the past nineteen and a half months. It has been a challenge, but I am so grateful for how you love on me and show me your love and presence.

As we are moving forward in this grief journey, I am finding that I am not as lonely as I have been. With that, please keep me safe from craving to be with someone. Protect my heart until you are ready to introduce me to that special guy. When it is time, please help us to honor you in our own relationships with you, and then us as a couple, to honor you.

Love you, Abba!

Your daughter,
Kimra

So Many Struggles

> Do not forsake me, O Lord! O my God, be
> not far from me! Make haste to help me, O Lord,
> my salvation! (Psalm 38:21–22)

I had experienced many struggles before, with the loss of my parents, grandparents, a cousin, a brother, an uncle, and many friends; but the struggles that I was about to experience with the loss of my beloved, Dwight, were going to be overwhelmingly hard and emotional.

The first thing I did was make sure that the kids got whatever of Dwight's that they wanted. I would not suggest doing what I am about to share. I pushed the kids to take stuff, just because I wanted it gone. It hurt too much to have reminders of Dwight all around me. For the first two months, every time they came over, I would offer them things. I would text them and call them, asking them if they wanted this or that. After a while, they conceded, "Mom, we don't need or want anything else." I understood.

In my journal dated May 7, I wrote that my friend Kathy came for a visit. I mentioned I had Dwight's clothing in my car to take to Goodwill. She offered to take them for me, which made me feel a little lighter. I was so grateful she offered. However, when I saw her take the first bag from my car, I bawled. Sending Dwight's clothes to Goodwill was just another reminder that he wasn't coming back to me. I asked God to wrap his arms around me and give me strength.

Lori and I had a counseling session that afternoon. I cried a lot—it was so hard! All the emotions of sadness and hurt poured out. I shared with her that I was in such a fog that my brain wasn't functioning. Lori reminded me that this was a normal byproduct of grief, as uncomfortable as it was. After all, Dwight had only been gone for three weeks by that time. "How long does it last?" I silently asked God. He reminded me that in his perfect timing, I would heal.

About two months after Dwight passed, I started having a hard time looking at my wedding band. It brought sadness, tears, and times of staring off into space. It felt heavy. It became hard to wear. My sweet love had fulfilled our wedding vows, until death do us part. After counsel from my sisterhood (Kathy, Becky T., Trisha, Janet, LouAnn, and of course, Lori), I decided to take my wedding band off. I opened my jewelry box and said, "Thank you for the best fourteen years of marriage. I am so glad to have been your wife." I kissed the ring and placed it next to his wedding band. Then I closed the lid. That is how I grieved the end of our amazing marriage.

Dwight and I had two vehicles. He drove a small red pickup truck that was a standard, while I drove an automatic SUV. Since I couldn't drive his pickup, our oldest got the truck. I was happy that it could stay in the family. It brought me comfort. My SUV was a lease in Dwight's name. I asked my son-in-love Caleb to go with me to return the vehicle. The gentleman who helped me was so kind. I shared why I was returning it, and he gave me his respects. He too was a veteran, so he brought me the license plates which had "Army Vet" imprinted on them. That was so sweet of him. The whole time I sat there, I was able to hold it together on the outside, but on the inside, my stomach was hurting, and I really just wanted to leave. Once Caleb and I did leave, I cried so hard as we walked past the car. I paused for a moment to take a picture of the last car we had together.

Dwight and I bought our four-bedroom, bath-and-a-half home on a quiet cul-de-sac in November 2015. We quickly became friends with all our neighbors. We all enjoyed making our yards look nice with flowers and yard decorations.

Spring came that year, and we started working on the yard, pulling out shrubs, taking down trees and cleaning up the flower beds. Dwight always said, "You work outside when it is nice out and inside when it is raining or snowing." And that is what we did. We renovated the house for the next seven years. Our fingerprints and footprints were all over the house. The house became a home to us and over five hundred guests through Airbnb. Our upper floor could house up to five guests at a time. During those four years, we were blessed to make many new friends.

After Dwight died, my heart, soul, and body struggled to be in the house. I tried different things to not deal with what I was going through. I would leave the house early, stay busy, take trips, etc. When I was home, I would sleep, change up the rooms, or pack up more of Dwight's things. I would cry, lying on the floor, or go for walks. I realized that I missed Dwight's presence. I missed not having him there to walk in the back door yelling, "Wilma, I'm home!" It just wasn't going to happen. I needed to accept this reality and remember all the laughter and love that we shared in our home. At times like this, I would turn to God to ask for his help and strength.

In July, three months after Dwight's passing, I packed his collection of hard cast trucks, most of our pictures, and the things on his dresser. I put our family pictures and his things from the bedroom in the living room to make the bedroom mine. I just wanted to make the heartache go away. Later that evening, I laid on the floor and bawled for twenty minutes, as I talked to my Abba. I asked him to wrap his arms around me. I missed Dwight and it hurt so much! As my tears slowed down, my body felt lighter. I went from lying on the floor, to sitting up on my knees, to standing. Then I started to sing and praise the Lord, "Thank you, Lord, for saving my soul. Thank you, Lord, for making me whole. Thank you, Lord, for giving to me thy great salvation so rich and free!" I found that in the midst of my sorrow, praising God warmed my soul.

One of the harder struggles I didn't anticipate was taking Dwight's phone number off our phone plan. I had been texting and calling that number for fifteen years! It was like a stab to my heart. My last text to him was on April 22, 2021, at 11:22 a.m. "Thank you for loving me the way you did! Enjoy being in Jesus's presence. I will be with you one day. BLYS XO."

Several months had gone by when Dwight's official death certificate arrived. I drove over to the funeral home to pick it up. When I got home, I sat down and read it. Tears pricked my eyes. Just seeing it made it so final, once again—my loving husband was dead and not coming home to me.

Hearing Dwight's name gives me comfort, but for some reason, it was hard and continues to be hard for some people to talk about him. After talking with family and friends, I discovered that they were worried that it would be hard on me. Once I shared how much I loved keeping his memory alive, people were willing to share. Please don't hesitate to tell your family and friends whether or not you want to talk about your loved one. I assure you that they will be supportive of your wishes.

Two years have gone by, and I still struggle to see the couch Dwight built for me. I also still struggle when I see Dwight's things and our pictures. That is why those things are at my daughter's. Maybe one day I can bring them back and smile when I see them. The couch is at a dear friend's home until I am ready. I am so grateful to have the support of my family and friends as I walk through my struggles, even two years later.

Struggles are just that—struggles. They will be temporary, but our Heavenly Father has you now and forever. Lean on him. Call out to him. He will hear you.

Grief

Jesus wept. (John 11:35)

Grief...what is it? The definition from Oxford Languages is "deep sorrow, especially that caused by someone's death." Following are two examples found in the Bible.

In the Old Testament, Job loses his children, workers, and livestock. Job 1:20–21 says, "Then Job arose and tore his robe and shaved his head and fell on the ground and worshiped. And he said, 'Naked I came from my mother's womb, and naked shall I return. The Lord gave, and the Lord has taken away; blessed be the name of the Lord." Job grieved and wondered why these things had happened, but he trusted the Lord and never turned from him.

In the New Testament, John 11:35 states, "Jesus wept." The Dr. David Jeremiah Study Bible notes, "When Jesus saw the tears of Mary and her friends, he wept, responding both physically and emotionally as he identified with their sorrow. The Lord sees and feels the anguish of God's people when their loved ones die."

Grief takes a toll on your body physically, mentally, and spiritually. For me, physically I lost twenty-five pounds. I wasn't eating well and sometimes not at all. My hair was falling out and I was drained. Mentally, I couldn't remember why I walked into a room. I would go back where I came from, asking God to help me remember what I was going to get. Most of the time, as I walked back to the room, I would remember. Then I would thank the Lord for helping me. I also battled foggy brain. Sometimes I would just sit in my chair and stare. Spiritually, I clung to my Heavenly Father as I knew that was best for me. I would listen to Christian music, read God's Word, hang out with other believers, and attend church. The only way to heal well and heal well for God was to immerse myself in God.

Grief is so different for each person. What I described are just a few things that I went through. I do know that if you have accepted Jesus as your Savior, you grieve differently because you know that you will see your Christian loved one again in heaven. This doesn't mean that you heal more quickly or that there is a how-to guide for overcoming grief. It doesn't mean that the trials you walk through are easier. It just means you know that God is with you in your trials. You also have the confidence that you will be with your Lord and Savior eternally. Knowing these things brings comfort.

I will say grief gets lighter with time. My body no longer hurts all the time and my heart doesn't feel like it is going to break. My brain fog has also lifted. However, it doesn't mean that I don't experience a wave of sadness when I miss Dwight. In those times I sit down, look at some pictures, shed some tears, and thank my Heavenly Father for Dwight. I often will sing a song like "'Tis So Sweet to Trust in Jesus." It is totally okay to have these moments, but remember to run to the Heavenly Father. He is ready and waiting to help you. You can cry to him, talk to him, wonder what is next with him, sit still with him, and then praise him for who he is—"The one who is the same yesterday, today, and forever" (Hebrews 13:8). He loves you and is always there for you.

In my journal dated Monday, June 7, 2021, at 11:24 p.m., I wrote:

> Abba,
>
> Grieving is so hard! It is a roller coaster of ups and downs, but I am grateful you are on this ride with me. Thank you for allowing me to share with people in a real way. I always want to show your love in all I say and do.
>
> Today I made this statement: "If some things could be settled, I wouldn't feel so heavily

weighted." Your timing is perfect; that weight is there so I will keep drawing closer to you, and for me to learn whatever it is you want me to learn and to give you glory. David cried out, "How long, oh, Lord?" And I wonder that same question!

Abba, the love of my life is with you, and I remind myself that Dwight is great. One day, I will be great when I am in your presence. But right now, I would just like to go from okay to good. All of me (my mind, body, heart, and soul) is still in the okay stage, and I long for you to just stay with me. Put a hedge around me so nothing can harm me—anything that will not allow me to do your work, loving others.

Thank you for the tears. They cleanse me and remind me how much I loved Dwight, and oh, how much I miss him!

You have allowed my grieving to be special to me, and I am trying to embrace it.

Thank you, Abba, for being there for me.

Love, your very sad daughter,
Kimra

Here is another excerpt from Mother's Day that year:

Happy Mother's Day!
Sunday, May 10, 2021, 11:14 p.m.

First, I am grateful to be a mom to my six children, their spouses, and others. Heavenly

Father, thank you for this blessing. You have been kind toward me, and I am honored and humbled. Each of these kids have truly been a joy (and also a challenge!). I am so grateful for my Heavenly Father's guidance in being a mom to them. I still need that guidance and help.

I attended church through the livestream on YouTube, due to still being under COVID quarantine. While singing, "I believe in the Father, I believe in the Son, and I believe in the Holy Spirit," I broke into prayer with a good cry, calling out for comfort. I verbally said, "I miss my love."

Missing Dwight has been more than my heart hurting and my body aching. Some days, missing him is not hearing his voice, (so thankful for his videos.) Missing him is not packing his lunch and making his coffee. Missing him is not feeling his touch or his lips for a kiss. Missing him is not being able to chat or watch YouTube and *Murdoch Mysteries* together. Missing him is not having him here to pick on me or at me. Missing him is us not building or working on projects together. Missing him is accepting that I am now the widow of the love of my life, Dwight Leroy Sutton.

Grieving is not something I have truly experienced. I guess I should make that clear. I have grieved for many loved ones, family, and friends, but this one is not easy. No matter what I do, rearrange the furniture or even move Dwight's things out, it doesn't make it any better. I have decided to slow down, take it all in, and be okay that the love of my life is part of this house and part of me. He always will be, and it is okay to grieve him.

The most important thing is to keep my Heavenly Father in the forefront of my thoughts and life.

"For God alone, O my soul, wait in silence, for my hope is from him. He only is my rock and my salvation, my fortress; I shall not be shaken. On God rests my salvation and my glory; my mighty rock, my refuge is God." (Psalm 62:5–7)

Thankful for my hope in you, Father. You are my rock and salvation. I will not be shaken because of you. My rest is in you, Father, my salvation and my glory. Father, you are my mighty rock and my refuge!

Amen!

On Thursday, June 24 at 11:33 p.m., I wrote:

Oh, today was so draining, emotionally and physically! I didn't realize how much I had bottled up missing my love. The things that I thought were no big deal became biggies! I realized them during my counseling session with Lori Z. Here are a few:

- Dwight always opened the bedroom curtains. I have not closed them since he passed away. Lori told me that I had to close them! One side is closed. Before I go to sleep, I will close the other side.

- I continually rearrange the furniture, but I wonder why, since Dwight isn't here. Half the time he never even realized it!
- Starting around 4:30 to 5:00 p.m., I have noticed that I start getting a little more emotional. That is the time Dwight used to come home.
- I do wonder sometimes why my Heavenly Father picked this time to take Dwight home to heaven. Asking questions is okay, as long as I follow them up with truth from scripture.
- "And we know that for those who love God all things work together for good, for those who are called according to his purpose." (Romans 8:28)
- Tomorrow, I go to get Dwight's death certificate. I am sure it will be another one of those moments. This is the certified one, the one with the cause of death listed. The other ones I have just said pending for cause of death.
- Another biggie is the fact that he is no longer next to me in bed. I am grateful for his T-shirt and his Cleveland Browns blanket.

Father,

I ask that as I am about to go to sleep, please turn my brain off, allowing my body, mind, and soul to relax so I can sleep. I want to be able to grieve well and give you all the *glory!*

GRIEF IN ITS JOURNEY

Thank you for being my shepherd, my guide, and my comfort. Thank you that you are the one who shows me new mercies every morning.

Your tired daughter,
Kimra

Precious Verses

> The Lord is near to the brokenhearted and
> saves the crushed in spirit. (Psalm 34:18)

As I have walked this grief journey these past two years, I have grown to lean on God's Word more and more. Some scripture I could readily relate to, such as Psalm 6:6–7a, "I am weary with my moaning; every night I flood my bed with tears; I drench my couch with my weeping. My eye wastes away because of grief." This was me for many months after Dwight's death.

Another verse I could relate to, on a more positive note, was Matthew 5:4, "Blessed are those who mourn, for they shall be comforted." My Heavenly Father heard and saw me mourn, and he comforted me with his Word, songs, and with family and friends. He was always giving me confirmation that I was his and would be okay.

Psalm 34:18 is so powerful: "The Lord is near to the brokenhearted and saves the crushed in spirit." The first two words, "The Lord," stand out to me. He is the one who will draw near to the brokenhearted. *Brokenhearted* can mean "distressed" or "discontent." I experienced both of these emotions in my newfound role as a widow trying to figure out who I was and what that looked like. Of course, first and foremost, I am a child of God, and I know that. However, with Dwight gone, I had to figure out what I would do without him. But, oh, the plans that God had and continues to have for me! He "saves the crushed in spirit." These words are amazingly sweet to me. When David penned these words, he was in a cave at Adullam. He was joined by desperate men. David was encouraging these men with Psalm 34. When I get to verse 18, it reminds me that no matter the despair I feel, my Lord will be near and save me.

Again, the first two words of Psalm 46:1 are so important. "God is our refuge and strength, a very present help in trouble." And what is he? Our refuge. *Webster's Dictionary 1828* has this to say about *refuge*—"shelter or protection from danger or distress." (This describes my Heavenly Father to a "T"!) As I have been working through my grief—the distress in my heart, soul, mind, and body—the Father has sheltered me from my own thoughts, as well as the words and actions of others toward me.

God is our strength. *Webster's Dictionary 1828* puts it this way: "support; that which supports, that which supplies strength, security." The Father has supplied strength daily, from the time I wake up to the time I go to sleep. I feel his support when I remember that his Son, Jesus, died on the cross for my sins, rose from the dead on the third day, and ascended to heaven. I receive support through the Holy Spirit. He is my helper through the valleys, on the mountaintops, and everywhere in between.

God is also a very present help in trouble. I have shared how I lie on the floor or my bed and cry so hard when I am missing Dwight. In those times, God has wrapped his arms around me. In 2018, I was diagnosed with essential tremors. This is a neurological disorder and is hereditary, however, it is initiated by physical, emotional, and mental stress. My tremors went into full gear after Dwight died. My hands, head, and torso would shake. Sometimes I lose my voice, and I have even had my teeth clatter. Regardless of the trouble I am walking through, my Father is a very present help. He is there to hear me, whether I am crying or laughing. He is there to give me the help I need.

"Be still and know that I am God" (Psalm 46:10a). This is a command. Be still. It's so important to stop and allow myself to be in his presence, to be in awe of him…and know that he is God. This reminds me that I serve a living God who can and will do anything for me, in accordance with his will. Sometimes I am down for weeks at a time. This is when I experience God's comfort and love. He wants me to rest in him through his Word. In the midst of my grief, he bids me to be still and bask in who he is.

These last two passages I share together because I praise God for his faithfulness in my grief. How could I not? My Heavenly Father has been my comforter, saved my crushed spirit, been near to me, been my refuge, my strength, and a very present help.

"But the Lord is faithful. He will establish you and guard you against the evil one" (2 Thessalonians 3:3). And finally, Psalm 34:1–3: "I will bless the Lord at all times; his praise shall continually be in my mouth. My soul makes its boast in the Lord; let the humble hear and be glad. Oh, magnify the Lord with me, and let us exalt his name together!"

My prayer is that as you read these verses, you will see who God is and know that he is with you as you walk your life's journey.

Songs

> Sing praises to the Lord, O you his saints,
> and give thanks to his holy name. (Psalm 30:4)

In my journey through grief, I have drawn close to my Heavenly Father by listening to Christian music. Words are so powerful! What you choose to listen to will set your mind on this world or on God in heaven above. In my sorrow, I felt so down, lost, and confused. I longed for joy in the Lord. I turned my focus to hymns, since many hymns were written out of sorrow, grief, and pain. I noticed that when I listened to or sang these songs, I would respond with uplifted head and hands, with tears of thanksgiving for my Heavenly Father's faithfulness.

I also included several Southern gospel songs as well as contemporary Christian music, some of which focused on heaven. When Dwight died and entered into the presence of Jesus, I longed to hear more songs about heaven. One such song is "How Beautiful Heaven Must Be" by Gloria Gaither. I listened to this song every night for about two months, starting with the night Dwight died. The comfort of knowing where Dwight was brought me peace.

King David wrote many songs, called psalms, from a heart filled with grief, sorrow, or pain. We see Psalms as a book of the Bible, but in David's time "it was a hymnbook of the Old Testament Jesus" (wikiversity.org; Music in the Bible [Psalms]). Today, music is put to scripture to direct us to who the Lord is. Psalm 33:1–3 (NIV) proclaims, "Sing joyfully to the Lord, you righteous; it is fitting for the upright to praise him. Praise the Lord with the harp; make music to him on the ten-stringed lyre. Sing to him a new song; play skillfully, and shout for joy." The following pages include some of my favorite hymns and what they mean to me.

Amazing Grace

[Musical score with lyrics:]

1. A-mazing grace! how sweet the sound! That saved a wretch like me! I once was lost, but now I'm found; Was blind, but now I see.
2. 'Twas grace that taught my heart to fear, And grace my fears relieved. How precious did that grace appear The hour I first believed!
3. Thru many dangers, toils and snares I have already come. 'Tis grace hath bro't me safe thus far, And grace will lead me home.
4. When we've been there ten thousand years, Bright shining as the sun, We've no less days to sing God's praise Than when we'd first begun.
5. A-mazing grace! how sweet the sound! That saved a wretch like me! I once was lost, but now I'm found; Was blind, but now I see.

Words by John Newton
Music by Early American Melody
PDHymns.com

"Amazing Grace" has long been my favorite hymn, from the time I was twelve years old.

Grace is the theme of this song. *Webster's Dictionary 1828* has this to say about grace: "the free unmerited love and favor of God, the spring and source of all the benefits men receive from him." Enduring Word shares this: "Grace is, by definition, the free gift of God, not given with an eye to performance or potential in the one receiving but given only out of kindness in the giver."

I love the fact that you and I don't have to do anything for God to show grace. He loves us for who we are.

Since Dwight died, I remind myself of this grace—unmerited love, the free gift and favor of God—when I am struggling with anniversary dates, a smell, a sound, the touch of Dwight's T-shirt, or eating his two favorite food groups, ice cream and chocolate! My God loves me so much that He brings others alongside me to walk through this journey of grief.

Amazing grace, how sweet the sound!

'Tis So Sweet to Trust in Jesus

1. 'Tis so sweet to trust in Je-sus, Just to take Him at His Word,
2. O how sweet to trust in Je-sus, Just to trust His cleans-ing blood,
3. Yes, 'tis sweet to trust in Je-sus, Just from sin and self to cease,
4. I'm so glad I learned to trust Thee, Pre-cious Je-sus, Sav-ior, Friend;

Just to rest up-on His prom-ise, Just to know, "Thus says the Lord."
Just in sim-ple faith to plunge me 'Neath the heal-ing, cleans-ing flood.
Just from Je-sus sim-ply tak-ing Life and rest, and joy and peace.
And I know that Thou art with me, Wilt be with me to the end.

Chorus

Je-sus, Je-sus, how I trust Him! How I've proved Him o'er and o'er!

Je-sus, Je-sus, pre-cious Je-sus! O for grace to trust Him more!

Words: Louisa M. R. Stead
Music: William J. Kirkpatrick
PDHymns.com

"'Tis So Sweet to Trust in Jesus" is a song that I have been singing since I was young. The chorus has stuck with me for the last ten years. For the past two years, I have clung to these words when I miss Dwight deeply. For about three months after Dwight died, I had what is called broken heart syndrome. I often sang this song out loud, crying and praising the Lord. "Jesus, Jesus, how I trust him!"

Blessed Assurance

1. Bless-ed as-sur-ance, Je-sus is mine! O what a fore-taste of glo-ry di-vine! Heir of sal-va-tion, pur-chase of God, Born of His Spir-it, washed in His blood.
2. Per-fect sub-mis-sion, per-fect de-light, Vi-sions of rap-ture now burst on my sight; An-gels de-scend-ing bring from a-bove Ech-oes of mer-cy, whis-pers of love.
3. Perf-ect sub-mis-sion, all is at rest; I in my Sav-ior am hap-py and blest; Watch-ing and wait-ing, look-ing a-bove, Filled with His good-ness, lost in His love.

Chorus

This is my sto-ry, this is my song, Prais-ing my Sav-ior all the day long; This is my sto-ry, this is my song, Prais-ing my Sav-ior all the day long.

Words by Fanny J. Crosby
Music by Mrs. Joseph F. Knapp
PDHymns.com

"This is my story, this is my song. Praising my Savior all the day long."

I love these words! God and I have been through a lot together in the past thirty years, but Dwight's passing was the biggest challenge of my life. I was not walking away from the One who loves, cares, supports, and provides for me. He is my Rock, my Salvation, and my Savior. He has brought me through waves of grief, sorrow, and depression. He is healing my broken heart. I will praise my God all the day long!

It Is Well with My Soul

1. When peace like a river attendeth my way, When sorrows like sea-billows roll; What ever my lot, Thou hast taught me to say,
2. My sin— Oh, the bliss of this glorious tho't— My sin, not in part but the whole, Is nailed to the cross and I bear it no more;
3. *(faster)* And, Lord, haste the day when the faith shall be sight, The clouds be rolled back as a scroll, The trump shall resound and the Lord shall descend,

(cues: vs. 3 only)

Chorus

"It is well, it is well with my soul."
Praise the Lord, praise the Lord, O my soul!
"E-ven so" it is well with my soul.

It is well with my soul, It is well, it is well with my soul.

Words by Horatio G. Spafford
Music by Philip P. Bliss
pdhymns.com

Verse 1 of this song is so true: "When peace like a river attendeth my way, when sorrows, like sea billows roll; whatever my lot, Thou hast taught me to say, 'It is well, it is well with my soul.'"

When Dwight went home to be with Jesus, I reminded myself that my soul was well, because I have accepted Jesus as my Savior, just like Dwight had. My sorrow, like sea billows, rolls up and down. "I have walked through the valley of the shadow of death" (Psalm 23:4), but praise the Lord, it is well with my soul.

My grief lightens when the wave of sorrow rolls out. Truly, whatever my lot, "God is my rock and salvation, and I shall not be greatly shaken" (Psalm 62:2).

Jesus Loves Me

[Musical notation]

1. Je-sus loves me! this I know, For the Bi-ble tells me so; Lit-tle ones to Him be-long, They are weak but He is strong.
2. Je-sus loves me! He who died, Heav-en's gate to o-pen wide; He will wash a-way my sin, Let His lit-tle child come in.
3. Je-sus loves me! loves me still, Tho' I'm ver-y weak and ill; From His shin-ing throne on high, Comes to watch me where I lie.
4. Je-sus, take this heart of mine, Make it pure and whol-ly Thine; Thou hast bled and died for me, I will hence-forth live for Thee.

Chorus: Yes, Je-sus loves me; Yes, Je-sus loves me; Yes, Je-sus loves me; The Bi-ble tells me so.

Words: Anna B. Warner
Music: William B. Bradbury
PDHymns.com

"Jesus loves me! this I know, for the Bible tells me so."

I have sung the words of this song since I was three years old. I find comfort in this song, knowing that Jesus loves me. He left heaven to be born to Mary and Joseph. He walked this earth teaching about his Heavenly Father. He willingly died for us, being crucified on a cross with nails piercing his hands and feet. He took all our sins upon himself as the perfect sacrificial lamb. His Heavenly Father turned his face from him as he bore our sins on the cross. John 19:28–30 states, "After this, Jesus, knowing that all was now finished, said (to fulfill Scripture), 'I thirst.' A jar of sour wine stood there, so they put a sponge full of the sour wine on a hyssop branch and held it to his mouth. When Jesus had received the sour wine, he said, 'It is finished,' and he bowed his head and gave up his spirit." On the third day, Jesus rose from the grave. He is *alive!* Mark 16:19 says, "So then the Lord Jesus, after he had spoken to them (the disciples), was taken up into heaven and sat down at the right hand of God."

I continue to sing "Jesus Loves Me" to my grandchildren to share with them who Jesus is.

If you have never thought about accepting Jesus as your Savior, or you have and don't know what to do next, please contact me at kimrajsutton1970@gmail.com. I would love to chat with you!

Comfort

> Blessed be the God and Father of our Lord Jesus Christ, the Father of mercies and God of all comfort, who comforts us in all our affliction, so that we may be able to comfort those who are in any affliction with the comfort with which we ourselves are comforted by God. (2 Corinthians 1:3–4)

People oftentimes seek comfort in ways that are not healthy, like overeating, drinking alcohol, doing drugs, etc. In grief, people can turn to these or other things like shopping or binge-watching TV shows. I found myself shopping, eating, and binge-watching TV.

In one of my sessions with Lori, she reminded me of the scripture in 2 Corinthians 1:3–4, "Blessed be the God and Father of our Lord Jesus Christ, the Father of mercies and God of all comfort who comforts us in all our affliction, so that we may be able to comfort those who are in any affliction, with the comfort with which we ourselves are comforted by God." After she went home, I thought about these verses. I decided I would rather find comfort in the Lord and heal well for his glory, so I would be able to comfort others in their grief. Paul Tautges explains these verses well in his book, *A Small Book for the Hurting Heart*: "God's healing comfort is for you, yes, but not only for you. The healing grace you have received in the past and are receiving now, is forged in the furnace of pain in order to become a means of grace for others. God's comfort is meant to be transferable." He continues, "The comfort you are blessed to bring to the heart of others is the very same comfort you receive when you are comforted by God. In other words, without suffering loss and grief, you would not receive the comfort of God firsthand. You would have less authentic comfort to pass on to others. On the other hand, when you receive healing grace from the Father of mercies—while you so desperately need it yourself—you become a greater blessing to others. That is the apostle's point in the scripture above."

So what does it look like to be comforted by others? I received cards, and still do after two years, which is such a blessing. For several months, a friend and sister in Christ sent me a text in the morning with encouraging and comforting words, along with scripture. People would call me, check on me, pray with me, or just let me share what was on my mind. They would direct me back to God, his grace and his love.

My sisterhood (Kathy, Becky E., Becky T., and Trisha) would come over. They would talk with me about my struggles and missing Dwight. They would ask how I was doing or if I needed anything. We would cry, hug, and pray.

Janet and LouAnn were two of my friends who have had deep losses in their lives. We took short trips, ate meals, and watched movies together. We played games and talked about our loved ones. We shared God's comfort, cried, and prayed.

Janet spent every day or evening with me for eleven months from the day Dwight died. When we weren't together, we texted or called.

LouAnn and I started a widows' group in September 2021. We met two Fridays a month, walking through our grief and giving comfort to one another. This group continues to meet a year and a half later.

All I can say is *wow!* God showed up through my friends, family, and church family to bring me comfort.

Encouraging One Another

> Therefore encourage one another and build one another up, just as you are doing. (1 Thessalonians 5:11)

Have you ever thought about what encouraging one another looks like? This is what God's Word says in 1 Thessalonians 5:11, "Therefore encourage one another and build one another up, just as you are doing." The two verses prior to this one mention Jesus Christ dying for us and that we obtain salvation through him. They go on to say that those who have died before us, as well as those who are alive when Christ returns, will live with him. This is the basis for encouraging and building one another up.

In the midst of our grief, it's easy to get lost when we allow our emotions to take over. In that state, what we are thinking can be detrimental to our well-being. This is the time to be encouraged and built up through God's Word. We can find joy in fellowshipping with family and friends, and most of all, other believers. Recognize the emotions and acknowledge them; work through them and talk about them; journal and ask God to help you navigate them in a healthy way. But don't wallow in them!

Our thoughts are another area of struggle. First, you need to "take every thought captive to obey Christ" (2 Corinthians 10:5b). Then follow up by using your "sword of the Spirit, which is the Word of God" (Ephesians 6:17b) to replace your negative thoughts. I love the footnote in Dr. David Jeremiah's Study Bible regarding this verse: "The only weapon for offense in the Christian's armor is the Word of God. Two Greek words are commonly translated word in English: *logos*, which describes the Bible as a whole, and *rhema* (the term here), which refers to a particular 'saying of God' that has special application for a given situation. The Bible as a whole is an armory from which to select swords for specific battles. Jesus illustrated the use of the rhema of God in his victory over Satan in the wilderness (Matthew 4:1–11)."

When I am battling a discouraging thought, I can go to my Bible to pick a "sword" to help me fight it off. In this case, Philippians 4:2–8 are my "go to" verses for counsel on exhortation, encouragement, and prayer. In verses 2–3, Paul asks the church to help Euodia and Syntyche, ladies who had "labored side by side" with him. In verse 4 he says, "Rejoice in the Lord always; again I will say rejoice."

With pen and paper, write down things you can rejoice about in the Lord. Here is a list that Dr. Jeremiah suggests in his Study Bible:

- His Word, Matthew 13:20; Luke 8:13
- His Birth, Matthew 2; Luke 1–2
- His Miracles, Luke 13:17
- His Suffering, 1 Peter 4:13
- His Resurrection, Matthew 28:8; Luke 24; John 16
- His Gospel, Acts 20; Philippians 1:18; 2; 3 John 3–4
- His Forgiveness, Matthew 18:13; Luke 15:6–10; 2 Corinthians 7:9
- His Spirit, Romans 14:17; Galatians 5:22–23; 1 Thessalonians 1:6
- His People, Philippians 2:2; 1 Thessalonians 2:20; 3:9
- His Vengeance, Revelation 18:20
- His Glory, Romans 5:1–2

In verse six of Philippians chapter four, we read, "Do not be anxious about anything, but in everything by prayer and supplication with thanksgiving let your requests be made known to God." Honestly, I have to remind myself of this even more in the midst of my grief. Anxiety is real, but God is real and bigger! I am learning to be encouraged through God and his Word, to pray as soon as I feel anxious. Verse seven continues with a promise when we pray: "And the peace of God, which surpasses all understanding, will guard your hearts and your minds in Christ Jesus." I love that my heart and mind will be guarded by the peace of God. In verse eight, Paul encourages us to think about these things: "Whatever is true, whatever is honorable, whatever is just, whatever is pure, whatever is lovely, whatever is commendable, if there is any excellence, if there is anything worthy of praise." When I look at these, it draws me back to the list of rejoicing in the Lord and who he is.

Encouraging one another is so important that God commands it in his Word. There is encouragement to be found in his Word. It is there for us to draw from, and help each other, whether walking through grief or life in general.

Prayer

> First of all, then, I urge that supplications, prayers, intercessions, and thanksgivings be made for all people. (1 Timothy 2:1)

When I think of prayer, I see it as a conversation with God. No fancy words—it can be short or long. Prayer can take place throughout the day or into the night. You can pray while you are standing, sitting, walking, lying in bed, driving, or biking; by yourself or joined by others. There is no limit to talking with God.

When I pray, I love praising God for who he is. For example, "He is the same yesterday, today and forever," according to Hebrews 13:8. And he is faithful. In 2 Thessalonians 3:3, it says, "But the Lord is faithful, and he will strengthen you and protect you from the evil one." I also love Psalm 62:1–2: "For God alone my soul waits in silence; from him comes my salvation. He alone is my rock and my salvation, my fortress; I shall not be greatly shaken."

Secondly, I give thanks for the Lord's provision for me, for my family, my friends and for another day to show his love to others.

After that, I pray for others. It brought joy to me to pray for others, even in my deep sorrow and hard grief. It took my focus off me and projected it onto others. In 1 Timothy 2:1, we read, "First of all, I urge that supplications, prayers, intercessions, and thanksgiving be made for all people." At times, I could not pray for myself. During those times I am so thankful that others were praying for me. Romans 3:26 states, "Likewise the Spirit helps us in our weakness. For we do not know what to pray for as we ought, but the Spirit himself intercedes for us with groanings too deep for words." I find it so comforting to know that the Holy Spirit "has my back." But the Holy Spirit isn't the only one interceding for us. Scriptures also tell us that Jesus intercedes for us. In Romans 8:34, it says that "Jesus is at the right hand of God and is also interceding for us." Jesus is called our "advocate with the Father" in 1 John 2:1. And Hebrews 7:25 tells us that Jesus lives to intercede for us. Wow! Just think! Jesus loves us so much that he is praying for us.

I like to end my prayer time with praise and thanksgiving. Sometimes I will sing a song to end my prayer time. One of the songs I like to end with is "Let's Just Praise the Lord."

As you have read through my pattern for prayer, I hope you will consider your own prayer life. Maybe you have never had a conversation with God, or maybe you have been conversing with him for five, ten, twenty years or more. No matter how short or long, create time to be in his presence. Grief can bring you very low, but talking to God has been the best thing to lift my spirits.

I love what 1 Peter 5:10 has to say: "And after you have suffered a little while, the God of all grace, who has called you to his eternal glory in Christ, will himself restore, confirm, strengthen and establish you." Thank you, God, for this promise!

Conclusion

One thing I have learned on this journey of grief is that there is no right way to grieve, no right amount of time to take. Grieving looks different for everyone.

However, I would encourage you to lean into it—to embrace it. But most of all, "Trust in the Lord with all your heart and lean not on your own understanding. In all your ways acknowledge him, and he will make straight your paths" (Proverbs 3:5–6). As you work through your grief, however it looks and however long it takes, trust God. Cling to him and he will guide you.

If you are struggling with suicidal thoughts or putting a plan into place to act on them, please stop, breathe, and call or text 988, the Suicide Prevention Lifeline. They are available twenty-four hours a day, seven days a week.

I highly recommend biblical counseling through a local church. I participated in biblical counseling for ten months after Dwight passed away. You may also want to consider participating in a Grief Share group. As I write this chapter, I am attending the first night of my second round of Grief Share. To find out more information, or to find a group near you, go to griefshare.org or call 1-800-395-5755.

I pray that as you walk your grief journey that, first and foremost, you will trust the Lord. If you don't know him, consider accepting Jesus as your Savior and sharing your decision with another Christian. Get the help you need through biblical counseling, Grief Share, or both. May your journey bring healing, glorify the Lord, and help others in their grief journey.

KIMRA SUTTON

The following is an entry from my Grief Study Week 9, January 4, 2023.

Worship God in your journal. Thank him for the relationship you had with your loved one.

> Abba,
>
> I bow before you in thanksgiving. I give you thanks for bringing Dwight into my life. You brought us together at your perfect time. You were so sweet to give us a year of friendship, a year to date, and just one month short of being married fourteen years.
>
> Thank you for helping us grow together in you. Thank you for teaching us to love each other every day as you love us. Abba, thank you for giving me Dwight—his sense of humor, his love for not only me, but for our six children and all our grandchildren, from little ones to adults.
>
> Thank you for his hard work, for his being a provider, for his love of flowers, for our walks and talks, and most of all, for the love he had for you. Thank you for his workmanship in building furniture for me. I treasure them now that he is with you.
>
> Abba, thank you for the gift of Dwight and the life we had together.
>
> Love, your daughter,
Kimra (and Dwight's wife)

Glossary of Terms

Sad (*Webster's Dictionary 1828*)

"Sorrowful; affected with grief; cast down with affliction."

As I walk on this earth, I find that I have been sad about many things. I experienced deep sorrow for several reasons during this journey. However, as I work through my grief, I draw closer to the Lord. There, I find comfort and peace, because my Heavenly Father is the same yesterday, today, and forever—the one constant in my life.

Pain (*Webster's Dictionary 1828*)

"n. (L. paena; Gr. penalty, and pain, labor); Uneasiness of mind; disquietude; anxiety; solicitude for the future; grief, sorrow for the past. We suffer pain when we fear or expect evil; we feel pain at the loss of friend or property."

I added spouse or family to that last statement. This definition touches the core of my body, soul, and mind. Pain is not just physical; it is grief and sorrow. It can take over through depression or sickness and hurt your soul. Pain is what I experienced when I found myself lying on the floor, crying, and calling on the God of compassion and love. I went to my physician and counselor to help me physically and mentally. My God provided for me in each of these situations. He can do the same for you, just call on him.

Suffering (*Webster's Dictionary 1828*)

"n. The bearing of pain, inconvenience or loss, pain endured; distress, loss or injury incurred; as sufferings by pain or sorrow; sufferings by want or by wrongs."

As I record the definition of *suffering*, it seems to me that it speaks of more than just grief connected to death. I have suffered in my body with my tremors, fibromyalgia, and asthma; however, grief has been the greatest of my sufferings. The following in 2 Corinthians 1:3–4 has been such a great reminder for me: "Blessed be the God and Father of our Lord Jesus Christ, the Father of mercy and God of all comfort, who comforts us, and all our affliction, so that we may be able to comfort those who are in any affliction, with the comfort with which we ourselves are comforted by God." I want to be able to comfort others in their afflictions as I have been comforted.

These next three words—*anger, anxiety, and fear*—are common to grief. But I'm not listing them in any particular order. Each emotion may be experienced many times, or you might find that you experienced only one or only once.

Anger (*Easton's Bible Dictionary*)

"The emotion of instant displeasure on account of something evil that presents itself to our view. In itself, it is an original susceptibility of our nature, just as love is, and is not necessarily sinful. It may, however, become sinful when causeless or excessive or protracted (Matthew 5:22; Ephesians 4:26; Colossians 3:8). As ascribed to God it merely denotes his displeasure with sin and with sinners (Psalm 7:11)."

Anger was one emotion I don't think I ever experienced, not that there couldn't be a time in the future. I never yelled or raised my fists, but I did cry out to God, "Why?" I thank the Lord for his graciousness to me in this area.

GRIEF IN ITS JOURNEY

Anxious (Oxford Language Dictionary)

"adj. Experiencing worry, unease, or nervousness, typically about an imminent event or something with an uncertain outcome."

Anxiety hit me when I found Dwight. My brain went into fight or flight mode. I got dressed and started talking to God about the list of things that needed to be done. This wasn't the only time I experienced anxiety. There were other times: planning Dwight's Memorial Service, taking back the leased car, buying another car, selling my house, packing, and moving across the country to the Adirondack Mountains of upstate New York, to name a few.

Philippians 4:6–7 are the verses I held on to and continue to hold on to: "Do not be anxious about anything, but in everything by prayer and supplication with thanksgiving, let your requests be made known to God. And the peace of God, which surpasses all understanding, will guard your hearts and your minds in Christ Jesus."

Fear (Webster's Dictionary 1828)

"A painful emotion or passion excited by an expectation of evil, or the apprehension of impending danger. Fear is an uneasiness of mind, upon the thought of future evil likely to befall us."

I experienced fear the first several nights imagining I would find Dwight dead in his recliner when I opened the bedroom door in the morning. After about three nights, I started singing "Jesus Loves Me" and reading Psalm 23 every night before bedtime, and the fear started to go away. Praise the Lord!

Remember, although grief is different for each of us, God's Word is still the strongest sword you can use to battle the negative emotions on your grief journey.

Sorrow (*Webster's Dictionary 1828*)

"n. The uneasiness of pain of mind, which is produced by the loss of any good, or of frustrated hopes of good, or expected loss of happiness; to grieve; to be sad."

Sorrow sprang to life in me at 6:55 a.m. on Thursday, April 15, 2021, when I found Dwight and discovered he was gone. I have experienced sorrow at other times in my life, but the sorrow produced by grief proved to be the hardest to walk through. I asked the question the psalmist penned in Psalm 13:2a many times: "How long must I take counsel in my soul and have sorrow in my heart all the day?" Psalm 88:9 says it this way, "My eye grows dim through sorrow. Every day I call upon you, O Lord; I spread out my hands to you."

God graciously reminded me, and continues to remind me, that he will "never leave me nor forsake me" (Hebrews 13:5b).

Heartache (*Oxford Languages Dictionary*)

"n. Emotional anguish or grief, typically caused by the loss or absence of someone loved."

About a month after Dwight died, I had my annual checkup. While my doctor and I were talking, I told him that my heart hurt so bad that it felt like it was going to break. He told me that it is a real thing. They call it "broken heart syndrome," and some people have even died from it! Then he said, "But you have a strong faith and friends and family who love you, so you will be okay!" To which I replied, "You're right—I will!" My heart no longer feels like it will break, but it does still feel sore at times when I experience the emotions of missing Dwight.

Forgive (*Webster's Dictionary 1828*)

"v. To stop feeling angry or resentful toward (someone) for an offense, flaw or mistake."

Forgiveness is so crucial to the grief journey—not only in forgiving the person who died, but also in forgiving yourself. At first, I looked back over my last four days on this earth with Dwight and asked myself, "Could I have helped Dwight more? Should I have noticed that he didn't look good or wasn't feeling well?" Asking such questions is futile and torturous. In the sovereignty of God, it was clearly in God's perfect plan to remove Dwight from this earth on that day and at that time. God is perfect, and we are not. We will never understand this side of heaven why God chooses to take our loved ones when he does, but we always know that he is good, and we can trust him.

Suggested Reading

- *A Small Book for the Hurting Heart* by Paul Tautges

- Christian Counseling and Educational Foundation

- *Grief, Finding Hope Again* by David Tripp

- *Grief, Learning to Live with Loss* by Howard A. Eyrich

- Resources for Biblical Living

- *Truth for Life (365 Daily Devotions)* by Alistair Begg

- *Finding Comfort as You Journey Through Loss, Grieving with Hope* by Samuel J. Hodges, IV / Kathy Leonard

Take Another Step

> The steps of a man are established by the
> Lord, when he delights in his way. (Psalm 37:23)

What was the next step? I had no clue how I was going to move, interact with others, or take care of myself, let alone take another step.

What I do remember saying to God is, "I want to heal well and heal well for you!" However, I really didn't know what that looked like. As time went on, he showed me it was taking another step forward. For me, that meant each and every moment of the day.

I trusted him and thanked him every day for whatever sleep I got. I would say, "Help me to take another step and show me what You have for me." He continues to do that even now.

No matter how hard it is to take another step, it is totally worth the energy. After each step, take a breath, thank God for his help, and embrace it. Taking another step will look different for each of us. Sometimes progress may be a tiny baby step, while another time a great big stride. The important thing is to take a step, whether small or large.

Be kind to yourself. If for some reason taking another step is too hard in that moment, rest, call a friend, listen to music, read a book, etc. Then, try again by calling on God and trusting he will help you.

Taking another step is what God wants us to do and what our loved ones in heaven would want us to do. They are the two best reasons to *Take Another Step*.

Dwight sitting on the couch he built, 2019, photo credit Kimra

Dwight and Kimra's wedding picture May 26, 2007, photo credit Cliff McGurk

Dwight and the flag he was proud to fly on our back deck, 2019

Dwight in his Cleveland Browns jersey and Kimra in her Dallas Cowboys jersey, October 2014, photo credit by ForHisGloryPhotography, Kathy Brady

Dwight, Kimra, Laura, Lindsey, Lauren, Victoria and Corey.
Taken 2008, photo credit, our niece, Bess Jones

Dwight and Kimra, taken in Oct 2014, photo credit
ForHisGloryPhotography, Kathy Brady

GRIEF IN ITS JOURNEY

Dwight and Kimra holding SuperHost sign made by Karina, one of our guests from Brazil. She stayed with us for 6 months. Taken in 2018, photo credit ForHisGloryPhotography, Kathy Brady

Dwight in his Cleveland Indians t-shirt and Kimra in her Detroit Tigers t-shirt, photo credit Nicole Garrett

Dwight and Kimra Oct 2014 photo credit
ForHisGloryPhotography, Kathy Brady

L to R…Kimra, Corey, Angie, Tori, Laura, Lauren and Lindsey. Taken Saturday, April 17, 2021 in the living room of Dwight and Kimra's home on Pleasant Court. I am so blessed to have these six children in my life and to be their mom.

About the Author

Photo credit Marla Lang

Kimra J. Sutton is well acquainted with suffering and loss. At the tender age of six, she lost her father to his battle with cancer. She is also a divorcee and later became a widow in April 2021. It was through the loss of her husband, Dwight, that this book was born.

Her heart belongs to her birth state, Ohio, but she currently resides with her husband, Milt, in Schroon Lake, New York, near her sister, Marla, and two of her six children and their spouses, as well as six of her twenty-five grandchildren, biological and blended in.

She has attended the Biblical Counseling Training Conference in Lafayette, Indiana, twice, as well as two thirteen-week sessions of Grief Share. Her heart's desire is to help others through their grief, showing them Jesus's love.